G000275715

THE
LITTLE BOOK
OF
BEREAVEMENT
FOR
SCHOOLS

THE
LITTLE BOOK
OF
BEREAVEMENT
FOR
SCHOOLS

Ian Gilbert
with William, Olivia and Phoebe Gilbert

Crown House Publishing Limited
www.crownhouse.co.uk - www.crownhousepublishing.com

First published by

Crown House Publishing Ltd
Crown Buildings, Bancyfelin, Carmarthen, Wales, SA33 5ND, UK
www.crownhouse.co.uk

and

Crown House Publishing Company LLC
6 Trowbridge Drive, Suite 5, Bethel, CT 06801, USA
www.crownhousepublishing.com

First published 2010. Reprinted 2013.

British Library Cataloguing-in-Publication Data
A catalogue entry for this book is available
from the British Library.

Print ISBN 978-184590464-7
Mobi ISBN 978-184590688-7
ePub ISBN 978-184590689-4

LCCN 2010930995

Printed and bound in the UK by
Gomer Press, Llandysul, Ceredigion

Contents

Five

School can be the place to escape from what is going on at home ('Home is home and school is school'). Respect that wish as much as possible

Six

Grieving is mentally and physically exhausting

Seven

Be tolerant of homework and other work commitments – evenings may well be spent grieving and talking, not working. Agree work commitments with the child, though, and be firm but caring as you try to ensure they don't get too far behind (and thereby add a feeling of failure to their grieving)

Eight

Talk to the spouse if they come to the school. Show them you know and care and are there to help. Don't just ignore them because you don't know what to say. That is more moral cowardice

Nine

Keep on talking to the child and letting them know you still remember, even just in small ways

Ten

Remember the anniversaries

Eleven

Be aware of areas you may cover in the curriculum that may bring back memories (Mother's Day, Father's Day, birthdays, life after death in RE, areas that touch on any illness such as cancer or mental illness and so on)

Twelve

When another parent dies in the school, make sure you are mindful of other children who have lost parents or indeed any loved one as it will bring many memories back

Thirteen

Learn about helping children to cope with bereavement from the various agencies out there

Fourteen

Time heals in bereavement as much as it does following an amputation. It is just what you go through to come to terms with things better

Fifteen

And thank you for taking the time to read this. You can make a terrible situation a bit less stressful for a grieving family

Foreword

This is a little book about a big thing. A thing that most adults assume children do not have to experience – the landscape of profound loss and change that we hope will not confront them until adulthood.

I meet bereaved children and young people at St Nicholas Hospice through Nicky's Way. This is an open access service to bereaved youngsters in our local area of West Suffolk. We also provide consultation and training to schools and other agencies.

The single most important message of the *Little Book* is the importance of giving your full attention to bereaved children in your school. Don't think there won't be bereaved children in your class because there will; you just may not know it. Indeed it is important to remember that for some children, the privacy of their loss is of paramount importance. Ideally, you and your school will know about the death of a parent, grandparent, brother or sister or any other special person to a child in your care. The most important response to a bereaved child is attending to what they say or indicate (through behaviour) as to how they are living with that death and what helps them.

Each child will grieve in a unique way, but knowing about grief and bereavement will help you help them – so please read this and anything else that gives you insight and courage. You will need courage, some knowledge and the backing of your colleagues to support a bereaved child in your class and school, but most of all you will need your humanity, tempered by professional skill.

This personal account gives you clear guidelines that will make a difference as to how a school supports a bereaved child in their midst and I want to thank Ian, William, Olivia and Phoebe for their courage in sharing so much. So be inspired by their courage and be brave and make death and bereavement in your school something that can be acknowledged and talked about. It would be really something if a child in your care could one day say, "When my Mum died, there was a teacher in my school who really helped me".

Yvonne Holman, Nicky's Way, Bury St Edmunds, Suffolk

Introduction

Of all the books I have written for teachers this one is the most personal. After a long illness, a mental illness (but that's a whole different book), my wife died on 11 June 2008. We had three children – my youngest daughter was then 9, my eldest daughter was 13 and for my son, the last time he saw his mother alive was on his eighteenth birthday, five days before she died.

This spread of ages meant that I was witness to the way that three entirely separate phases of educational institution tried and succeeded, tried and failed and sometimes didn't try at all to help my children come to terms with their loss.

Several months after their mother's death BBC's *Newsround* aired a brave and still controversial programme in which four children talked about their own losses. This prompted my children and me to sit down and think about how we could use the network of Independent Thinking schools to get across to teachers what they could do to help children who had lost a parent based on our own experiences. We did this by way of a fifteen-point PDF handout on one side of A4.

It was well received, including a request to translate it into Welsh for a conference later that year for teachers, social workers, school nurses and others who may be involved with children facing bereavement. I mentioned to the organisers that I would be prepared to come along and speak at the conference for free. My daughters volunteered to join me. One aspect of serious illness and bereavement is trying to make sense of it when there is, actually, no sense to be had. Drawing on your experiences to help others helps you with finding some sort of purpose to the chaos and awfulness.

The responses at this conference – 'We know we get it wrong at our school but we don't learn and then, when it happens again, we get it wrong all over again' – and the response to the e-mailshot of our resource from across the UK and further afield, prompted me to suggest to Crown House that maybe it would be worthwhile elaborating on the initial handout and producing a simple book for schools under Independent Thinking's *Little Book* series.

Which is what you now have in your hands.

Like I say, this time it's personal. It isn't other people's research. It isn't based on years of extensive study. Maybe what my children say they would have liked is not what everyone would want in a similar situation. We are all different. (Except that, when it comes to grieving, we all follow a fairly ubiquitous pattern of denial, anger, bargaining, depression and acceptance, according to thanatologist Elisabeth Kübler-Ross.) You can do the research on grieving yourself. And because it's personal, the main thrust of this book is from the perspective of a child who has lost a parent. That said, it may be that the suggestions can help a child dealing with any sort of serious loss. I just hope – my children and I just hope – that you will find advice in this book to help those children that little bit more. Their world has just fallen apart. The least you can do is read this.

One

As soon as the death is known to the school have a senior member of staff talk to the immediate classmates about what has happened. Stamp out any gossip and offer support for those who may be affected

Ignorance is a vacuum that gossip quickly fills. And gossip – lies perpetrated by people too lazy to wait for the truth and too shallow to want it anyway – is a very destructive force in anyone's life, let alone a child's, let alone a child's at this time.

What is more, gossip, tittle-tattle and fanciful invention quickly take root as received truths in the classroom, the playground, the staffroom and then in kitchens at home and from there on into the virtual social world that most children inhabit. So, while the child is away dealing with the end of their world as they know it, a whole tangle of lies is being created behind their back.

As if they don't have enough to deal with.

In my daughter's secondary school, one member of the senior leadership team was a personal friend. When I went to break the news to my daughter, and then take her home, I made sure that the office informed him of what had happened. I found out later that he had immediately called together my daughter's tutor group, informed them of the facts of the situation and with a seriousness and firmness that made a significant impression on the class, instructed them that he would not tolerate any gossip or rumour-mongering from them and that they would have him to deal with if he discovered any.

What he was also able to do at that moment by using his authority and his honesty, was to offer support to the students in my daughter's class who were genuinely upset by my wife's death, many of whom knew her personally.

To know that all this was being dealt with by him in such a professional, firm and caring manner was of huge benefit to my daughter as well as to me. It also gave a framework, a structure, that helped the other students know what to do and how to react in a situation where most adults don't know what to do or how to react.

I remember when I was 10 the father of one of my best friends died suddenly and again, before the gossip kicked in, our form tutor gathered us together and, fighting back her own tears, explained what had happened and what we were to do. I remember it clearly, even though it is almost thirty-five years ago.

Teaching is one of the most powerful jobs on the planet at the best of times. In dire times like this, done well, it has the potential to be one of the most dignified and supportive.

Two

Send a condolence card and encourage classmates to do the same. Saying 'I didn't know what to do' and doing nothing is a form of moral cowardice – and why should you be let off the hook? No one else knows what to do either

We received cards and e-mails from people every day and they stopped on the morning of my wife's funeral. At a time when what you are going through is incredibly personal and closed off from the world, such gestures are tremendously supportive and played a huge part in helping us through those first few numb, painful (and I know that is an oxymoron but that's how it is) days and weeks.

Within a day of my friend's actions at the secondary school we were receiving cards and flowers from my daughter's friends and the occasional, appropriate, visit.

My younger daughter was at a small rural infant school and, while I do not know exactly how the children were told about what had happened, within a day or so we received a bundle through the letterbox. Inside were cards designed and painted by every single child in the school addressed to my daughter and, although the messages were rather abrupt at times – 'Sorry your mum's dead. Gavin' – the heart was always in the right place. In terms of doing the right thing, they were *exactly* the right thing. In this way, not only did the children in the whole school have a structured way of responding to the situation, they also created something that made a difference to their classmate's life.

The infant school also sent a card from the head teacher on behalf of the staff, which was a lovely gesture – whereas the secondary school didn't because 'We didn't know what to do'. One or two of my friends acted in a similar way and I couldn't help but feel disappointed and let down by them. Nobody knows what to do. There is nothing you can do. Nothing anyone can do. But doing nothing is never the right thing to do. A card, an e-mail, a baked cake, a text, anything – no matter how futile you feel it may be – is better than nothing.

Ninety-nine per cent of the cards contained the words, 'Let me know if there's anything I can do'. It's a cliché but it's a start. One of the cards contained words to the effect, 'Rather than saying is there anything we can do we want to be specific about what we *will* do'. They then went on to offer us a weekend away at a time to suit us doing rock climbing and an assault course in the Cheshire countryside. We went several months later and it was *absolutely* the right thing to do. Doing the 'Leap of Faith' from the top of a pole thirty feet up onto a trapeze in the crisp November sunshine was something that my girls will never forget.

On the subject of what to do or not to do, a quick word about the funeral. Go! Unless there are specific instructions not to, ensure that at least someone suitable is there to represent the whole school such as a member of the management team or the tutor or the head of year or all three of them. Furthermore, encourage the classmates most affected by the loss to attend the funeral too if they are old enough, possibly going with a parent if necessary. Although the grieving family will probably not register who was actually there during the ceremony (it was the first time I had seen those special cards that the undertaker distributes, which each person fills in and leaves behind as a record of who was there), the feeling of support and love from a group of people who are all there for you and for the person you are all remembering is very powerful. My children's friends being there for them was as much a support for my children as my friends being there for me.

On top of that, remember that funerals serve a very powerful purpose in helping everyone to come to terms with the loss and get off the starting blocks as it were when it comes to grieving. Denial is so much harder when you have seen the coffin.

Three

When the child comes back to school talk to them (but don't patronise them). Ask them how they would like their teachers to act

Three

Sometimes coming back to school is the best thing the child can do – the first rung on the ladder to getting their life back again (although the ladder goes on forever). For some children, though, going back to school will feel like too much too soon. The problem is that maybe they won't know that until they get there.

When the child comes back you have to do everything you can to make sure that this will not be a normal day for anyone, not least the child, and then do everything you can to make sure it is a normal day.

Speak to the staff and let them know what is happening. In my experience, many will not know what to say and will either overlook the death (in my son's college, while the tutor was brilliant, the rest of his teachers simply ignored the situation) or just give sad, sympathetic looks that although probably well meant, don't help. The child doesn't need pity from adults; they need strength, consistency and understanding. And 'How are you?' is not a good question either. The child will probably reply with 'I'm fine' because they know that is what people want to hear but, in reality, they want to scream how it really is. A simple but sincere, 'I was really sorry to hear about the death of your mother' is fine. Another strategy is to deflect your sympathy towards another family member. 'How is your sister getting along?' or 'How is your father coping?' can be a useful way to show you care.

Sometimes people leap in with a story of their own loss. This is not helpful at this stage, or at least not if you divert the focus onto yourself entirely. Our experience was that we didn't want to hear anything about anyone else at this early stage of grief. It was an unnecessary annoyance and a selfish act by the perpetrator. 'I know how you are feeling because I went through it too at your age' can be useful and, at some point in the future, the child may want to come back to you on it so you can explore things further. But for now, use your experience to know what to do and what not to do. That is all you can do at this point.

Of course, the above is just our opinion based on our experience and you might find a child in your care thinks differently. You can always ask them. They may have an idea and that may well be 'Treat me normally' or they may have no idea at all in which case make sure you have a plan anyway. Part of this should also be ensuring that, at any time of the day, the child knows that they can just get up and go to a safe place without asking or explaining. This may be your office or an unused meeting room. Make sure that all staff know about this and if the child leaves part way through their lesson to let this happen without fuss or hindrance. Grief is like standing on a beach and being hit by waves. You don't know when they are going to hit you but you know they will and when you do there is nothing you can do to stop it. Make sure the child knows they can go to the safe place whenever they feel they want to and no one will make a big thing of it. In fact everyone will be really understanding. It might be that you nominate a friend to escort them there but then leave them on their own if that is what they want. Nominating that person in advance avoids the crush of girls if you ask, on the spot, for a volunteer or the awkward silence from the boys as they stare at their pencils.

Make sure all adults – teaching and non-teaching – are keeping an eye out for the child too and ensure that you are reassuring the parent that this is what is happening. To know that so many people are keeping a discreet and caring watch over your child at such a time is very reassuring for the parent and allows them to get on with their own life, such as it is, at the same time.

Four

Teach other children to know what to say and how to handle things

In my experience, most adults haven't got a clue how to act and what to say when someone has died, but then why should they? No one has taught them and, culturally, we treat death like Belgium. We know it's not far away but no one wants to talk about it let alone go there. If, as adults, we've gone through our entire lives avoiding facing up to it, then how does it feel for the children in your classrooms who suddenly have to deal with it?

The more you can talk about dying with the children, before a real-life death takes place in your school, the better, in my view. There are many opportunities for doing this, using vehicles such as RE, Circle Time, Philosophy for Children, PSHE and even History or English to share stories, explore beliefs and convictions and identify a common vocabulary for talking about death. From the death of someone famous to the death of a grandparent or the death of a pet, all of these are opportunities to start opening up about the topic in your school and starting to break down some of the taboos. This will make life just that little bit easier when (as opposed to 'if') something terrible happens at your school.

And when I say vocabulary I mean it, literally. Like John Cleese in the Dead Parrot Sketch, often people can't even articulate the word 'dead' and so resort to that great British habit of the euphemism. Telling a class that so and so's father has 'gone to sleep now' is not helpful to anyone except you (although better than 'pushing up the daisies' or 'fallen off his perch'). That said, 'has died' is less brutal than 'is dead'.

Give the children some examples of what they could say such as, 'I'm really sorry to hear about the death of your ...' or 'I'm really sorry. You know I'll always be there for you.' Make sure they don't put any undue pressures on the grieving child to be either happy or sad. My children have been asked repeatedly in the two years since their mother's death why they weren't crying, the implication then arrived at by simple childish logic being that their mother can't be dead then. As if they were making the whole thing up. The first time this happened my youngest came home very distressed. They deal with it better now after we talked it through but they still come home with the occasional, resigned, 'It happened again ...'

Let the children know that, at times the child will want to be alone, at times they will want their friends around them, at times they will seem happy, even laughing, at times they will suddenly burst into tears or go off in a rage. Let them know that such changes can happen very quickly and that they are perfectly natural. Don't let them think that if the grieving child is laughing then they have forgotten. Or if they are crying that they should be given a hanky to make them stop. Crying is good, natural and useful. And can't be stopped anyway. The classmates need to learn what it is to be an unconditional friend at this stage, being there for the grieving child no matter how they act and react.

Five

*School can be the place to escape from
what is going on at home
('Home is home and school is school').
Respect that wish as much as possible*

As anyone who has taught children from troubled backgrounds (which is all of you) should know, sometimes schools can be the only safe, reliable, consistent place in their world. Yet the new convergence of social care, parental involvement, health support and education means that school's place as a haven of normality and an escape from the troubles and tribulations of life at home is under threat.

During the period before my wife's death there was a great deal of stress and distress at home. Any family dealing with serious illness, especially a terminal one (and yes, I include mental illness in that list) will experience this. For many teachers, they have no idea what sort of scenario that child comes from and returns to each day. The fact that they turn up on time, washed, in uniform, with their homework even partly done is a testament to that child's resilience and determination to be, well, normal.

While some children may need support at school to deal with all that the world is throwing at them at that time, others may not want it. It could be that such an intrusion may be detrimental to their well-being. My younger daughter benefited hugely from the opportunities she had to sit down and talk one-to-one with the visiting school nurse and we are all extremely grateful for the professional, unconditional, non-judgemental support she gave my daughter. Time with this nurse was the safe place my daughter needed both before and after her mother's death, the nurse herself providing something concrete and anchored in a world that was becoming neither.

My elder daughter, however, was very different. She used school as a way to 'forget' all that was going on at home. The phrase 'Home is home and school is school' is one of hers and it was her way of surviving the ordeal of the illness and her mother's death. School was where she could be normal and she needed that very much. Whether the difference is an age thing or just a reflection of the difference in their personalities I cannot say. But there is a difference and you cannot have a one-size-fits-all policy in such matters.

How will you know which one to apply and when? Firstly, ask the child. Secondly, liaise with the parent. I certainly knew which was the preferred strategy of my three children. Thirdly, use your professional acuity. Keep your eyes and ears open. And fourthly, keep asking (without nagging) so that the child knows that there will be help as soon as it is needed at school. They only need to ask.

Six

Grieving is mentally and physically exhausting

Have you ever watched a weepie movie and come out of the cinema all limp and exhausted? Being emotional takes up a great deal of physical and mental energy. Now imagine crying like that day after day for weeks. And the times you are not crying are because you are in too much pain to cry – and you wish you would cry because it makes you feel a little better, but not much – or because you are asleep. Although then you often wake yourself up crying. Or wake up after a lovely dream where everything was as good as it used to be and then, as the reality of your new bereavement hits you, you just want to go back to sleep but you can't. So you cry.

Grieving is an incredibly tiring process, as exhausting as it is relentless in the early days and weeks. Your body clock is out. Your daily routines are out. Your appetite is out. Your sleeping patterns are out. Your whole cycle of sleeping, waking, working, resting and everything else associated with daily life has been turned upside down and inside out and you feel you will never be normal again.

What's more, the process of grieving can – should – involve a great deal of talking. It certainly did in our house. And talking about what has happened and how everyone is feeling will find its own time and place and is no respecter of bedtimes. Especially when, for the child, going to bed is the worst time of day, the time when they feel most alone.

What this means is that the child may not be particularly alert in class, may not have done their homework, may not even be able to stay awake in a particular lesson, may not be able to concentrate, may be irascible or erratic, or any manner of indicators of someone who is overwhelmingly fatigued.

Having somewhere, then, that child can go if they just need to grab a quick nap when they suddenly feel the need is very useful (and as sleep is such welcome respite from being awake at a time like this it is a shame to waste it). Reinforcing with other staff members that the physical demands of grieving mean that the child may not have finished their homework or be up to that game of sport or want to go out and play is useful too. Ensure that the child is eating as well as possible. They may not be eating at home or even having the opportunity to eat with all that is going on. They may not even want to eat at lunchtime so having a sandwich put by for them and letting them eat it part way through the afternoon may be beneficial.

The key here, as with so much of helping children who are grieving, is staying alert and being flexible. Keep an eye on what their needs are and then respond to those needs as creatively and quickly as possible without making a fuss.

Your professionalism, though, also demands that you find a balance here as you will see in Chapter Seven.

Seven

Be tolerant of homework and other work commitments – evenings may well be spent grieving and talking, not working. Agree work commitments with the child, though, and be firm but caring as you try to ensure they don't get too far behind (and thereby add a feeling of failure to their grieving)

Your homework on the rain cycle, for example, will not be top of a bereaved child's list for a while so you must be tolerant. For those children who are using school to escape the distress of what is happening at home, it is when they leave the school gates that the work really starts.

As I mentioned above, evenings and nights will be spent grieving in whatever shape that takes. If the child is fortunate, it will take the form of plenty of love and cuddles and talking. Speaking honestly, openly and without being judged is so important at this stage. The taboo nature of death, not to mention the other baggage that many families carry with them, means they never actually communicate and can remain trapped in a terrifying Pinteresque world. It means that often the death is not talked about and the remaining parent may well become 'stuck', unable to let go, unable to move on, unable to be of any real support to their children. This leaves the child lost and alone as they try to deal with their own feelings, which means that there is even less chance of them being able to concentrate on their school work.

Falling behind at school or college will make a bad situation worse, especially if the child is in key stage 4 or 5. What are you going to do to ensure that the child has the space and time to grieve without undue pressure to make their brain do things it can't yet do, like concentrate or remember things or care about that homework on the rain cycle but, at the same time, exert just enough pressure to make sure that the child stays, if not on track, not too far from it?

My son was similar in his approach to my elder daughter when it came to keeping home and college separate as much as possible, although the nature of an FE college is more hands-off anyway on the whole. However, he had a tutor who would speak to him often, who spoke to me as was necessary and whom we both knew was there if we needed her. In this relaxed but caring way she steered my son through his time at the college, putting just enough pressure on him to achieve the grades he was capable of without letting him off the hook and using his home life as an excuse for not handing in work. She also knew when to ease back and just be there for him as a sad and lost young person, not just a student.

One morning my son and I went in to college together and sat down with her as she went through every one of his assignments and outlined where he was, how far behind he was, what he needed to do to catch up and what scores he needed to achieve his target grades for each area. The three of us left that meeting with a copy of this sheet, a plan and sense of reassurance that it was achievable. My son knew exactly where he stood and what he had to do. He also knew that, although he was the one who had to put in the work, he was not alone.

Eight

Talk to the spouse if they come to the school. Show them you know and care and are there to help. Don't just ignore them because you don't know what to say. That is more moral cowardice

The bottom may have fallen out of the child's world following the death of a mother or father, but it is not a
bed of roses for the surviving partner either. If that parent
then makes the effort to come to school, to show his or her
face when all they really want to do is curl up and join their
spouse, as the awful dawning that the responsibility for their
children lies entirely in their hands now, no longer shared,
then the least you can do is to be supportive.

My elder daughter went back to school the week following
her mother's death, partly as a result of her 'school is school
and home is home' strategy and partly because it was
Activities Week so there were no 'normal' lessons as such.
During that week she became involved in a big musical pro-
duction with a presentation to parents on the Thursday. If
she had the strength to do this then the least I could do was
go along and support her. She had lost one parent; I don't
want her ever to feel she has lost both.

As the crowd of parents and children edged their way
through the double doors of the school sports hall where the
performance was being held, my daughter's head of year was
standing at the entrance welcoming in parents. As I passed,
even though I was inches from her, she could not bring herself to look at me, much less speak to me. Once inside, sitting
there amongst a crowd of strangers, I felt like the most alone

person in the world, like the empty eye of a hurricane, cut off, lost. On the way out I saw the head teacher who became too emotional too talk and just looked at me with tears in her eyes. At least she looked me in the eye. I was overwhelmed with a need to get out of there and so rudely pushed my way through the crowd and back into the summer evening air. I just wanted to collect my daughter and go back home to our sad, safe space.

So, what can we learn from that evening? When you are grieving, getting out of bed is an ordeal let alone attending a school play, so be mindful of the enormous effort the parent is making and the strain they are under. The head of year later told my teacher friend that she felt really bad but didn't know what to say. *She* felt bad! As I say in the chapter title, doing nothing is moral cowardice. However hard it is for you it so much harder for them, so just get on with it and 'do your day job' as they say. And being emotional yourself is OK. It shows empathy and connection.

And if you see them sitting in the school hall looking lost and alone just go up to them, touch them on the back and say a simple, 'You must be so proud of your daughter, Mr ...' or 'She's done so well hasn't she? And don't worry, we'll keep an eye on her' or something equally caring, acknowledging and reassuring.

As a footnote to this chapter, what support are you able to engineer for the grieving parent from other parents who may have gone through the same loss? In the school car park, as I was hurrying myself and my daughter home after the performance, I met a woman who had a girl in the same year as my daughter who had lost her husband in tragic circumstances several years earlier. She was the first person to call on me after the news broke of my wife's death and she remained in contact in just the right way afterwards. In the car park she introduced me to her 'new' husband (they had been married for several years but 'new' sounds so much better than 'current'). She knew what it was like and, importantly, she was able to reassure me that life goes on, that happiness returns, that things will get better, that I would find love again. She was right.

Nine

*Keep on talking to the child and
letting them know you still remember,
even just in small ways*

Talking is like Germolene. It takes the pain away a little bit and helps just a little bit and gives you something to do while the real healing process is taking place. And it is so much better than doing nothing. Make sure the child has every opportunity to talk about what has happened and their feelings about it not just immediately after their parent's death but in the weeks, months and, if possible, years after the tragedy.

There are two magic ingredients here too – having somewhere to talk and having someone to talk to.

As I mentioned above, my younger daughter had her school nurse and she continued seeing her a couple of times a week for as long as she could, including when she moved to middle school a few months after her mother's death where the nurse picked up the reins again.

My elder daughter went once to the school nurse and that was all she needed. Although she could have seen her at school the policy of keeping home and school separate meant that she did not want this. Instead we arranged the visit at the local doctors' surgery where they spent an hour or so talking. Although my daughter was happy to go she didn't feel she wanted to do it again and that was fine by me. At least she knew the school nurse's face and where the door was and that the door would always be open and the face would always be kind.

During this visit, the nurse described to my daughter a useful way to understand the difference between the way small children grieve and the way older children and adults mourn. Adults, she explained, grieve in rivers where they are fully immersed in their grief for an extended period of time following a death. Little children, on the other hand, grieve in puddles. In other words, the child moves in and out of their grief like someone stepping in puddles. Sometimes they are fine. Sometimes terribly, albeit briefly, sad. It was a really helpful analogy and even now my younger daughter will talk about having 'puddle moments' or a 'puddly day' where things have all got too much for her again. We help her through it by listening supportively and then we all know it will pass, till the next time.

Sometimes the chat you need is not an in-depth, soul wrenching, open all the floodgates, better out than in heart-to-heart. You just want someone to say, 'How is it going now?' or 'How is your father/brother/sister getting on?' or 'What are you planning for your holidays this year?' Something that starts a conversation about day-to-day life without the deceased parent and that shows you haven't forgotten and that you care. Even, if well timed, 'What do you miss most about your mother?' can be useful and, you may be surprised to learn, doesn't always lead to tears.

Sometimes people worry about mentioning the deceased person's name in case the bereaved relative has forgotten and they don't want to open up the wound again and make them cry. If the only thing you learn from this *Little Book* is the following then it will be worthwhile:

The bereaved person *never* forgets about the person they are missing and the fact that you mention them by name means that person is still, in some way, alive. Because of this it is *always* the best thing you can do. And if it makes that person cry, it doesn't matter. Crying is not wrong. In fact, it is amazing how much daily life can be conducted with tears streaming down your face.

Ten

Remember the anniversaries

When you are grieving time is a double-edged sword. On the one hand it seems to stop and you are desperate for it to get going again so you can make a start on rebuilding your life. On the other hand, like dropping someone off at a bus stop, the further on you travel, the further from them you end up. Suddenly you cannot recall their face or the sound of their voice or their smell and you begin to realise that your story is now being written in which that person who was everything to you is now just a name and an emotion. No more.

But once every 365 days things change.

The anniversary of the death, especially the first one, is a very difficult time. Especially if it is linked to other anniversaries, as in my household, the last time my three children saw their mother or the last time I saw my wife, which was several days before her actual death.

For the first anniversary I took all three of them out of school and college for the day. Although none of the establishments had a problem with this, I did still have to fill in a 'holiday form' from the secondary school and, supposedly, obtain the head teacher's permission to do this. Surely there must be a form that can be filled in for absence that does not say 'holiday' on the front and make you feel like you are doing your child's education a terrible disservice by taking them out for the day? Anyway, we went to London to see the matinee performance of *Les Misérables* as part of our 'better out than in' policy. I wanted to address the grief head on and spend the day together but not moping. (As a surprise I then bought them tickets for *Billy Elliot*, thinking something a bit more light-hearted at the end of the day would help. I forgot that Billy had lost his mother. And then there was the 'Dear Billy' song ... Talk about exhausting. But anyway, like we say, better out than in.)

Make a note in your diary of the anniversary of the death and, on the day, make contact with the child somehow to let them know you know. If you let other staff know too that will help both in terms of watching out for the child during the day and also letting them know that none of you have forgotten.

And to show you really care, don't just remember the first anniversary. Although they become less painful with the passing of time (so we're told) the anniversaries over the coming years are still days of heightened emotions and intense memories. We are now coming up to the second anniversary but still, last night at the dinner table, my youngest was in tears telling me that she didn't want 11 June to come around again.

Something to bear in mind here is the question of transition. While my son and my elder daughter were at the same educational establishment on the first anniversary of their mother's death, my youngest had changed schools. She had gone from her infant school to a middle school but from there to a primary school because we had moved house. Despite explaining the situation to the primary school head teacher and the class teacher they just didn't get it and never engaged with my daughter and her grieving. Maybe it was because they had not lived through the drama and the trauma of my wife's death and its impact on a school or maybe it was because they just didn't really care about their children in the way that I know other schools would have done. Who knows? Either way, the first is an excuse and the second is unforgivable. I remember speaking to my Independent Thinking associate and friend Julie Duckworth who is a primary head teacher and the author of *The Little Book of Values*. She would have been 'all over' my daughter and her grieving in a highly caring and supportive way and was appalled at the lack of interest shown by my daughter's primary school (and don't get me started on Mother's Day! That's for the next chapter ...).

To what extent are you aware of the particular situation of the children joining your school and what anniversaries are there to watch out for? And if the child is leaving your school, what can you do to ensure the new school 'gets the message'? These are vital questions for you during transition or handover between schools and ones you need to get right.

Eleven

Be aware of areas you may cover in the curriculum that may bring back memories (Mother's Day, Father's Day, birthdays, life after death in RE, areas that touch on any illness such as cancer or mental illness and so on)

'We won't be doing anything special on Mother's Day,' said my daughter's primary school teacher. I was surprised by this response to my question about the day. I just wanted her to be aware of what had happened, that it would be my daughter's first Mother's Day without a mother and to tread thoughtfully. It seemed reasonable to me and although I was surprised by the response – I thought all primary schools made a fuss of Mother's Day, churning out paper bouquets and cards with pictures of kittens on them like they were going out of fashion – I went away reassured that I had the event covered.

However, the Friday before Mothering Sunday my daughter came back from school looking very subdued and so I asked her what was wrong. She said that her class had been to a 'special' assembly where the deputy head had waxed lyrical about how wonderful mothers are and how the children should take really good care of them. 'OK,' I said, not quite sure what to say. 'So, how was that?' 'It was really embarrassing,' she replied sadly. 'All my friends kept turning round and looking at me and asking if I was alright, but I didn't want them to,' she explained.

Thanks, Miss Whatever Your Name Was of Class 5!

Yes, I know schools are busy places and there is always lots going on but I would have thought it possible for my daughter not to have been put in that position. What can you do at your school and across your curriculum to deal with such situations with a little more tact and understanding? Are you vigilant on Mother's Day, Father's Day, anniversaries and birthdays for children who may be that little bit more fragile on such days? The last thing we are suggesting is that you don't bother with such events (or rename them 'Surviving Carer's Day') or even exclude the grieving child from them. Just give them warning. Show you are thinking. Show the child – and the parent – you care.

And it is not just such annual events to watch out for - dealing with life after death in the RE curriculum or dealing with illnesses in areas such as Biology or tales of loss in English. All of these can be approached with sensitivity but not soppiness. In my son's college, before a lesson that was going to touch on issues to do with mental illness, his tutor discreetly took him to one side and explained what the topic was going to be. She gave my son the choice of not attending or sitting there without joining in or of joining in as he saw fit. She made it clear that if at any point he felt he needed to leave then that would be fine. No questions asked. What she did, apart from taking away that awful element of surprise that the grieving person has to deal with on a daily basis, was to give him choice. And at a time in a young person's life where they feel there is so much that is out of their control, with all the concomitant levels of stress such a situation generates, she had given back to him the reins to his life. Wonderful!

Eleven

My son then went into the lesson and joined in with some of his own experiences in a mature, balanced, un-mawkish way.

Honestly, it is not that hard.

Twelve

When another parent dies in the school, make sure you are mindful of other children who have lost parents or indeed any loved one as it will bring many memories back

According to the Child Bereavement Charity, fifty-three children a day lose a parent in the UK. Winston's Wish, the UK's leading child bereavement organisation, suggests that the figure is nearer 24,000 children a year having to come to terms with losing a parent. That is one bereaved child every 22 minutes.

Add that to their statistics that 3,000 young people each year die as a result of accidents or serious illness, that seventeen babies a day will die at or soon after birth and that 6,000 families a year are affected by suicide, and you know that sooner or later, probably sooner, you will have to deal with a child at your school dealing with such an issue. And then it will happen again, to another child.

If you have acknowledged the various suggestions from our own experiences in this book as well as made use of the training and resources offered by the various organisations listed in the resources section then well done. However, apart from mobilising yourself for the newly bereaved child you need also to look over your shoulder at the recently bereaved.

In my middle child's school within a few months of my wife's death another mother died, and in similar circumstances. How the school handled the particular girl who was in my daughter's year I do not know. She had also lost her father several years before and I think she ended up in care. While I would want the school to do everything it could to support the bereaved child it would have been helpful for someone, maybe the class tutor or the head of year, to have had a quiet, discreet word with my daughter to see how she was too.

Again, I know that schools are busy places and that, as institutions, they do tend to have short memories. Life goes on relentlessly and SATs, exams, parents' evenings and training days come and go like the passing of the seasons. Yet, if you want to show that being a caring school is more than just a motto for your prospectus between 'putting people first' and 'bringing out the best in every child' then these are the areas in which you have to prove your mettle.

Thirteen

Learn about helping children to cope with bereavement from the various agencies out there

This book is just a personal view from first-hand experience about what schools can do – and should not do – to help a grieving child. But it is just one tool in a whole arsenal of support available to all professionals who are in the position, whether they like it or not, of supporting a young person through the worst time of their life.

From what I have seen there is no expectation that there should be a whole-school policy on supporting a grieving child and training seems to be down to the individual rather than something that is addressed by institutions. However, sending someone on a course offered by the sorts of organisations listed in the resources section of this book, buying a few resources and maybe having the teacher not so much 'cascade' what they have learned as 'distil' it into a few key points that are easy to grasp, easy find amongst all the other school bumph when you need to (and as we saw in the previous chapter, you *will* need to) and easy to perform, would be a half-day's training very well spent.

Remember, of course, that amongst your staff there will be those who are also recently bereaved or who perhaps also lost a parent when they were at school. The same rules apply to them as apply to the child in Chapter Eleven. If the situation is handled sensitively they will have a great deal to offer their colleagues in this element of their professional development.

The majority of these organisations offer support packs and resources as well as provide training for the whole school or for a nominated individual. Winston's Wish, named after the Winston Churchill Fellowship that founder and clinical psychologist Julie Stokes was granted to study childhood bereavement in the US and Canada in the early 1990s, has even teamed up with Teachers TV for a video showing how professionals from their organisations helped children from a primary school and a secondary school come to terms with their respective losses.

There may well be other, more local support on offer too. We were living in Suffolk when my wife died and, through the Family Carers support we were receiving anyway, we were put in contact with a local hospice, St Nicholas in Bury St Edmunds. They ran a bereavement support group specifically for children called Nicky's Way and in the months following our loss, all three of my children benefited from spending time with Yvonne (who wrote the foreword to this book) who supported them in a professional, effective and knowledgeable way. It is because of this support – entirely free to us – that all proceeds from this book will be going to Nicky's Way.

One simple procedure you can put in place immediately is to nominate a room, near reception, that can be used to break bad news to a child. In my daughter's infant school the head teacher was away so we were ushered into her office while the secretary went to find my daughter. It was a small school so it was a process that did not take very long. In my elder daughter's secondary school, however, I had to ask for a room we could use which turned out to be the head of year's office – several twisty, endless corridors from the main reception area where my daughter had been brought to me. That was a long, long, hurried walk, leading my daughter by the hand as she followed in agitated silence, fearing the worst. Yet I know that the school had various rooms and offices behind the main reception area that would have served the purpose just as well. When the ashen-faced parent turns up in your reception and asks for their son or daughter to be brought out of class to tell them the news, what will your procedure be to make that awful event slightly less traumatic and problematic for those concerned?

Whether you look to local support offered by a hospice or a church group, to the large national organisations such as Winston's Wish or Cruse or even international ones such as Rainbows, be assured that you will be learning invaluable insights and approaches. You may not know when they will be called upon but you can be certain that day will come in some shape or form. Then you will know that it was time and money well spent.

Fourteen

Time heals in bereavement as much as it does following an amputation. It is just what you go through to come to terms with things better

Fourteen

Time, they say in bereavement as with many of life's traumas, heals. But healing implies getting better, going back to how it was, being as good as before. In bereavement this is not the case. It never goes back to how it was before. It never goes away. Life gets better, not because of the absence of the pain, but because you learn to live your life despite it.

One woman my girls and I met at the Welsh conference I mentioned in the introduction suggested that we see grieving like a 'pebble in your pocket'. It is always there. It is uncomfortable at times. It sticks into you when you least expect it. But at times you can get it out and hold it, look at it, deal with it in your hands. And it is painful and distressing but at least it is real and tangible and concrete, and you want to cry and you do cry, but then you can put the pebble back in your pocket, until the next time, and get on with your life.

My wife's brother died in an accident when he was 19. Being on the edge of a distraught family in this way showed me that what grieving individuals want most is to talk about the person who has died. And that does not go away with time. My wife still suffered terribly at the anniversary of her younger brother's death and also on his birthdays. I have since seen this with other people I have met who have been bereaved. I talk to them about the person they have lost and, without fail, they thank me for it. Why? Because everyone else skirts round the subject and would rather talk about the weather than the person who has died, would even rather cross the road than talk about that person. Remember, just because the person is not weeping inconsolably does not mean they have forgotten or that time has 'healed' them. It simply means they are not weeping inconsolably at that moment. They will again. Then they'll stop again. That is the way it goes. So, if you are worried about not talking to someone about their loss for fear of upsetting them, don't worry. They are upset anyway, just hiding it. And talking to them will help. Why? Because talking about the person is the only thing that keeps that person alive, that's why.

As I mentioned in Chapter Four, both of my daughters have been approached by young children who take them through the same sort of childish logic:

Child: *Is it true your mum has died?*

My daughters: *Yes.*

Child: *I think you're lying.*

My daughters: *No, it's true.*

Child: *Well, why aren't you crying then?*

My daughters: *It doesn't work like that. Now go away ...*

So, when it comes to supporting the grieving child in your class or in your care, keep at it. Be there for them for the long haul. Show them you care by remembering to show them you care on an ongoing basis. Remembering is so important to them now. It is all they've got of the person they've lost. Do your bit.

Fifteen

And thank you for taking the time to read this. You can make a terrible situation a bit less stressful for a grieving family

Fifteen

I'm sorry if I have come across as a little blunt in some of my views over the course of this *Little Book*. I guess seeing your children being unnecessarily upset at a time when you need all the support you can get to help them can make you rather grumpy.

For those of you who have read this far, though, may I – may we – thank you for taking the time to do so. Nothing can take away the pain of the loss the children are dealing with. But your actions – little ones, whole-school ones, genuine ones, professional ones, personal ones – can and will make an awful scenario just that little bit easier to deal with. And in doing so you will help the parent know that, when his or her children go back to school in the days or weeks after the tragic day, they will be cared for and supported in a way that actually counts and allows the whole family to start the process of picking up the shattered pieces of their lives and moving on.

And for that we thank you.